Illustrations copyright © 1992 by Dorothée Duntze

Published in the United States by North-South Books Inc., New York.

Published simultaneously in Great Britain,
Canada, Australia and New Zealand by North-South Books,
an imprint of Nord-Süd Verlag AG, Gossau Zürich, Switzerland.

Library of Congress Cataloging-in-Publication Data
Twelve days of Christmas (English folk song)
The twelve days of Christmas / illustrated by Dorothée Duntze.
Summary: On each of the twelve days of Christmas,
more and more gifts arrive from the recipient's true love.
1. Folk songs, English—England—Texts. 2. Christmas music.
[1. Folk songs—England. 2. Christmas music.]
I. Duntze, Dorothée, ill. II. Title.
PZ8.3.T8517 1992
782.42′1723′0268—dc20 91-32359
ISBN 1-55858-151-0 (Trade binding)
ISBN 1-55858-152-9 (Library binding)

British Library Cataloguing in Publication Data
Duntze, Dorothée
Twelve Days of Christmas
I. Title
782.28 [J]
ISBN 1-55858-151-0

3 5 7 9 10 8 6 4 2
Printed in Belgium

The Twelve Days of Christmas

ILLUSTRATED BY Dorothée Duntze

North-South Books / NEW YORK

On the first day of Christmas
My true love sent to me
A partridge in a pear tree.

On the second day of Christmas
My true love sent to me
Two turtle doves,
And a partridge in a pear tree.

On the third day of Christmas
My true love sent to me
Three French hens,
Two turtle doves,
And a partridge in a pear tree.

On the fourth day of Christmas
My true love sent to me
Four calling birds,
Three French hens,
Two turtle doves,
And a partridge in a pear tree.

On the fifth day of Christmas
My true love sent to me
Five gold rings,
Four calling birds,
Three French hens,
Two turtle doves,
And a partridge in a pear tree.

On the sixth day of Christmas
My true love sent to me
Six geese a-laying,
Five gold rings,
Four calling birds,
Three French hens,
Two turtle doves,
And a partridge in a pear tree.

On the seventh day of Christmas
My true love sent to me
Seven swans a-swimming,
Six geese a-laying,
Five gold rings,
Four calling birds,
Three French hens,
Two turtle doves,
And a partridge in a pear tree.

On the eighth day of Christmas
My true love sent to me
Eight maids a-milking,
Seven swans a-swimming,
Six geese a-laying,
Five gold rings,
Four calling birds,
Three French hens,
Two turtle doves,
And a partridge in a pear tree.

On the ninth day of Christmas
My true love sent to me
Nine drummers drumming,
Eight maids a-milking,
Seven swans a-swimming,
Six geese a-laying,

Five gold rings,
Four calling birds,
Three French hens,
Two turtle doves,
And a partridge in a pear tree.

On the tenth day of Christmas
My true love sent to me
Ten pipers piping,
Nine drummers drumming,
Eight maids a-milking,
Seven swans a-swimming,
Six geese a-laying,
Five gold rings,
Four calling birds,
Three French hens,
Two turtle doves,
And a partridge in a pear tree.

On the eleventh day of Christmas
My true love sent to me
Eleven ladies dancing,
Ten pipers piping,
Nine drummers drumming,
Eight maids a-milking,
Seven swans a-swimming,

Six geese a-laying,
Five gold rings,
Four calling birds,
Three French hens,
Two turtle doves,
And a partridge in a pear tree.

On the twelfth day of Christmas
My true love sent to me

Twelve lords a-leaping,

Eleven ladies dancing,

Ten pipers piping,

Nine drummers drumming,

Eight maids a-milking,

Seven swans a-swimming,

Six geese a-laying,

Five gold rings,

Four calling birds,

Three French hens,

Two turtle doves,

And a partridge in a pear tree.